US STEEL: THE RISE, FALL, AND RESURGENCE OF A GLOBAL GIANT

HARPER STERLING

Contents

Chapter 1: About US Steel

The American steel industry was thriving in 1901, thanks to the country's growing urbanization and infrastructural development. A strong financier, J.P. Morgan, saw a chance to consolidate the industry's fragmented terrain. He oversaw the consolidation of numerous major steel corporations, notably Andrew Carnegie's Carnegie Steel Company, to become the United States Steel Corporation (U.S. Steel).

At its peak, United States Steel controlled over two-thirds of American steel output. It was critical to the industrialization of America, supplying steel for railroads, skyscrapers, bridges, and numerous other projects. The firm also exerted tremendous political and economic power, earning both praise and condemnation for its monopolistic dominance.

The Great Depression of the 1930s had a significant impact on US steel, as steel demand fell. Labor upheaval, government inspection, and stiff rivalry from overseas producers all posed challenges to the corporation. It went through many restructurings and divestments, getting rid of non-core businesses and streamlining operations.

In 1986, US Steel underwent a major transition, forming USX Corporation, a holding corporation. USX expanded its business beyond steel by investing in oil and gas, chemicals, and real estate.

Global steelmakers, notably those from Asia, rose to prominence in the late twentieth century, able to produce steel at reduced costs. Due to intense competition, US Steel proceeded to restructure, closing plants and laying off workers.

USX broke off its core steel operations as a separate publicly traded corporation in 2002, renaming itself United States Steel Corporation. This change enabled US Steel to concentrate completely on steelmaking and improve its competitiveness.

U.S. Steel has made great achievements in modernizing its processes, investing in new technology, and improving efficiency since its spin-off. The corporation has also benefited from the American industrial sector's revival and increased steel prices.

However, the steel industry in the United States continues to face issues, such as variable steel pricing, trade disputes, and the constant need to adapt to technological improvements.

Chapter 2: US Steel's Trials and Tribulations Through the Decades

US Steel's tale, like the metal it forges, is one of strength and endurance, but also of great pressure and long-lasting wounds. It was a symbol of American industrial supremacy for decades, with its furnaces blazing throughout the twentieth century. However, the road was not without bumps, with multiple crises, challenges, and a slow decline that continues to define the sector today.

J.P. Morgan merged several companies in 1901 to become US Steel, which grew to control about two-thirds of the US steel market. However, it had difficulties even in its early stages. Labor unrest, particularly the Homestead Strike of 1892, drew public attention to the harsh realities of working conditions. Antitrust concerns led to a 1911 Supreme Court order that separated the corporation, even though it remained a dominant influence.

The mid-twentieth century proved to be the golden age of US Steel. The corporation expanded abroad, diversified its product lines, and became a cornerstone of the American economy, fueled by wartime demands and burgeoning domestic industries. Steel was the foundation of infrastructure, buildings, automobiles, and a plethora of other things, and US Steel was the king of its castle.

However, the seeds of deterioration were sown during this time. Globalization and the rise of foreign competitors, particularly from Japan and Korea, resulted in lower-cost, frequently higher-quality steel. US Steel struggled to adapt because of legacy infrastructure, unionized labor, and environmental legislation.

The 1970s were a watershed moment. Steel demand was hit hard by the oil crisis and the economic downturn. Foreign imports increased as a result of currency manipulation and unfair trade practices. Closures, layoffs, and bankruptcy became the norm. The term "Rust Belt" was coined to describe the devastation in steel-dependent towns.

US Steel experienced a number of problems. It was on the verge of bankruptcy in 1982, only spared by government credit guarantees. Further reduction and restructuring occurred in the

1990s, with mergers and acquisitions becoming the norm.

US Steel is still a prominent participant today, but its dominance is a distant memory. Its market share has declined drastically, and the industry landscape has shifted dramatically. Mini-mills, which are small and efficient, have dominated the market. Concerns about sustainability and the environment have introduced additional problems.

Chapter 3: An Unsolicited Bidding War Heats Up

U.S. Steel, the American steel titan, was in the midst of a scorching furnace - an uninvited bidding war that has the industry and investors sweating. The Pittsburgh-based multinational is navigating a complex terrain of potential suitors and regulatory challenges after rejecting a $7.3 billion buyout offer from rival Cleveland-Cliffs.

Cleveland-Cliffs, North America's largest iron ore producer, stunned the industry in October 2023 with an unsolicited $33 per share cash offer for U.S. Steel. This bold initiative sought to establish a local steel giant, controlling about half of the flat steel market and perhaps posing a monopoly threat in several important areas.

The board of directors of US Steel quickly rejected the offer, citing antitrust issues, probable job losses, and undervaluation of the company. However, the refusal did not put out the fire. Rumors of additional potential suitors, including foreign steel titans, started to circulate, keeping the bidding battle hot.

Chapter 4: Steel Giant Nippon Steel Digs Deep for U.S. Dominance in $14.9 Billion Acquisition of U.S. Steel

Nippon Steel, Japan's steel manufacturing powerhouse, has agreed to buy its American equivalent, US Steel Corp., for a whopping $14.9 billion. This bold move, backed by a smart mix of opportunity and acumen, positions Nippon Steel to overtake China's Ansteel Group as the world's third-largest steel manufacturer.

The transaction plays out like a chess master's gambit. Nippon Steel, which is currently ranked fourth in the world, has meticulously harnessed a confluence of factors:

1. **Government-Fueled Resurgence**: The Biden administration's ambitious initiatives, the Infrastructure Investment and Jobs Act and the Inflation Reduction Act, are shaping America's industrial environment. These legislative pillars provide enticing tax incentives, creating a healthy setting for home industry resurgence. Nippon Steel was acutely aware of this transition, anticipating an increase in steel demand due to infrastructure spending and industry reshoring.

2. **Competitive Advantage through Consolidation**: The rich history and established footprint of the U.S. Steel in the American market, together with Nippon Steel's global reach and technological prowess, create a powerful synergy. The United business will dethrone Ansteel and propel Nippon Steel to the

world's third medal place, with an estimated yearly production capacity of 58.56 million metric tonnes.

3. **Financial Allure**: Nippon Steel is providing $55 per share in cash, a hefty 40% premium above US Steel's pre-deal pricing. This sweetens the transaction for US Steel shareholders, making it even more appealing.

Nippon Steel's action is more than just an acquisition; it is a determined step toward cementing its global dominance. Nippon Steel is prepared to rewrite the global steel scene, engraving its name even deeper in the annals of industrial titans, by leveraging on America's reindustrialization surge and strategically integrating U.S. Steel's assets.

Chapter 5: Union Pushes Back on Nippon Deal

The United Steelworkers union has voiced significant opposition to Nippon Steel's proposed acquisition of US Steel. Despite Nippon's assurances that all existing labor agreements will be followed, the union is suspicious and vows to "protect the good, family-sustaining jobs we bargained for."

This stance puts the arrangement in jeopardy, as the union represents a sizable chunk of US Steel's workforce. Their fears derive from previous experiences and a lack of trust in Nippon's commitment to labor accords.

Nippon, on the other hand, is upbeat. They point to their successful union relationships at Standard Steel and Wheeling Nippon Steel as proof of their dedication to fair worker practices. They also expect the transaction will face no regulatory or antitrust challenges.

Chapter 6: Nippon Steel of Japan

Nippon Steel Corporation (NSC) is a multinational steelmaker based in Japan. After ArcelorMittal, it is the world's second-largest steel producer. Yawata Iron & Steel and Fuji Iron & Steel merged to form the company in 1971. NSC employs over 70,000 people and operates in over 40 countries.

Nippon Steel produces a wide range of steel products, including:

- Steel plates
- Steel sheets
- Steel bars
- Steel pipes and tubes
- Stainless steel

- Titanium
- Steel slag

Products from the company are used in a wide range of industries, including:

- Construction
- Automotive
- Shipbuilding
- Machinery
- Energy
- Infrastructure

Nippon Steel is committed to sustainability and has set aggressive targets for lowering greenhouse gas emissions. The corporation is also investing in new technology research and development, such as improved high-strength steel and hydrogen-powered steelmaking.

Nippon Steel plans to invest $4.5 billion in a new steel mill in Vietnam by 2023. The facility is scheduled to begin production in 2026 and will have a capacity of 2 million tons of steel per year.

Nippon Steel is a prominent player in the global steel business, and it is dedicated to providing high-quality, environmentally friendly steel products. The company's investment in new technologies and commitment to sustainability will secure its position as an industry leader for many years to come.

Chapter 7: Strategic advantages

The merger of Nippon Steel Corporation (NSC) with United States Steel creates a steel industry giant ready to redefine innovation and quality. This strategic partnership sparks a symphony of synergies, promising:

1. **Technological Harmony**: Both sides' cutting-edge expertise fuses, accelerating breakthroughs in high-grade steel products such as electrical and automotive flat items. This digital crescendo of shared knowledge pulls the combined company to the forefront of steelmaking developments, ensuring clients throughout the world benefit from this harmonious blend of know-how.

2. **Sustainability as the Score**: The relationship is infused with a forceful green note thanks to U.S. Steel's Big River Steel, a masterwork of eco-conscious engineering. Synergies can be found by improving operations, increasing energy efficiency, and advocating for recycling, resulting in a harmonious balance of production and environmental responsibility.

3. **Improved Melody in America**: The domestic reach of U.S. Steel, along with NSC's long-standing presence in the U.S. market, creates a perfect harmony to meet the expanding demand for high-grade steel. Customers will be serenaded with a broad choice of premium steel goods, painstakingly created to fit their changing needs, ranging from automotive to electrical applications.

4. **A Strong Future Composition**: NSC's dedication to the US market ensures consistent delivery of high-performance steel products, with each note reflecting quality and dependability. This collaborative orchestra of expertise, creativity, and environmental conscience has the potential to create a powerful symphony for the future of steel.

5. **Hydrogen Harmonies**: NSC brings their ground-breaking hydrogen injection technology for blast furnaces, while U.S. Steel's electric arc furnaces contribute their eco-friendly tune. They form a potent duo, lowering carbon emissions and paving the way for cleaner steel production.

6. **Electric Arc Ensembles**: The mini-mill maestro of US Steel joins NSC's orchestra of expertise, increasing the repertoire of sustainable

steel solutions. These electric furnaces sing a lovely melody of energy efficiency, cutting the industry's dependency on fossil fuels and lowering its environmental footprint.

7. **Direct Reduction Divas**: The industry's rising star joins forces with both companies to develop next-generation direct iron reduction technologies driven by hydrogen. This clean and efficient technology has the potential to rewrite the steelmaking score by removing carbon emissions from the iron manufacturing stage.

Chapter 8: Unveiling the Details of the Nippon Steel-U.S. Steel Merger

The historic merger of Nippon Steel Corporation (NSC) with U.S. Steel has made the global steel sector. Beyond the headlines, however, is a complicated web of financial maneuvering and logistical problems. Let's go into the nitty gritty of this historic transaction:

1. **The Value Symphony**: The agreement values US Steel at $14.9 billion, demonstrating the combined entity's potential as a steel behemoth.

2. **Shareholder Serenade**: Shareholders of US Steel will get $55 in cash per share, making this a lovely symphony for investors.

3. **Regulatory Rhythms**: The acquisition is scheduled to close between April and September 2024, subject to shareholder approval and customary regulatory approvals.

4. **Banking on Brilliance**: In order to finance the acquisition, NSC has obtained large loans from a consortium of Japanese banks, expressing their confidence in the merger's success.

5. **No Funding Hesitation**: Unlike many mergers, this one is not predicated on obtaining extra funding, which adds a degree of confidence to the process.

6. **Debt Management**: Managing the combined entity's acquired debt will be critical to its long-term financial sustainability. Careful

planning and effective debt management will be essential for securing a financially stable future.